GONDOLIN PRESS

Francis Templar

THE CITY ABOVE

THE MOUNTAIN

The contemplative life at an epic change

Introduction by Ado Maria Valli

gondolin press

THE CITY ABOVE THE MOUNTAIN – *Francis Templar*

Original title: *La città sopra il monte* (2019)
© Fede & Cultura (Italy)
www.fedecultura.com

Editing: Kevin Chan

© gondolin press
1331 Red Cedar Cir
80524 Fort Collins CO

www.gondolinpress.com
info@gondolinpress.com

2018 © Gondolin Institute LLC
ISBN 978-1-945658-14-3

All the literary and artistic rights are reserved. The rights for translation, electronic storage, copying and total or partial adaptation, by any equipment, (including microfilm and photostats) are reserved for all countries. The Editor remains at disposition for eventual holders of rights who have not been traced.

First edition: October 2019
Printed in USA

Introduction

by Aldo Maria Valli

Dear reader, I have to warn you: if you, like I imagine, are a faithful Catholic, belonging to Holy Mother Church, the pages that follow will provoke in you a profound disturbance.

The author puts his finger in a sad and shocking wound.

In the course of the bimillenary history of Christianity, more than once it has happened that the contemplative monastic life was under attack by the part of hostile forces. Now however, for the first time the attack comes explicitly from the inside of the very Church, even from its leadership. It is an attack that takes place, in the name of a poorly understood concept of "renewal" by two official documents: the Apostolic Constitution *Vultum Dei quaerere* on the contemplative female life (from 2016) signed by Francis and the Applicative Instruction of the Apostolic Constitution, *Cor orans* (from 2018), emanated by the Congregation for the Institutes of Contemplative Life and Societies of Apostolic Life.

In what does the attack consist? Said in few words, it consists of a tentative to disfigure the contemplative life, to make it closer not to God but to the world.

Rightly the author observes that these two documents have caused "great disturbance, perplexity and sufferings in many institutes of female contemplative life." Because there are Sisters that, in light of faith and tradition, have come to understand the imminent risk and all are faced in front of a lacerating choice.

"The Church lives of the Holy Ghost" affirmed the author quoting Saint Paul VI. The Church is in fact "a continuation of the miracle of Pentecost". This is why, as Saint John Paul II reminds us,

> *In the Dogmatic Constitution on the Church (the Lumen gentium), the Second Vatican Council declared that the consecrated life, in its multiple forms, manifests the infinite power of the Holy Ghost, admirably working in the Church.*

The renewal of the consecrated life can thus only come under the impulse of the Holy Ghost. However, *Vultum Dei quarere* (VDq) does not mention this fact. Why? Because the idea of renewal that it is subject to does not coincide with rising towards holiness, but to an adaptation to the logics of the world.

Saint Paul VI already well understood the danger. It was 1969 when, in a speech to hundreds of religious superiors from all over the world, he warned that renewal, for those who had chosen the religious life, cannot have any objective other than that of presenting to the world, in the most faithful way possible, the very face of the Lord. If instead with the term "renewal" one intends surrender to mundane mentality and the tendency to pander to "transient and changeable styles and behaviors, to camouflage with the world in its forms, without discernment and without criteria" then we do not have a renewal but a betrayal. "If salt loses its taste, with what can it be seasoned? It is no longer good for anything but to be thrown out and trampled underfoot" (Mt 5, 13).

We know that secularization is unfortunately well infiltrated also in many great religious orders, but it is exactly because of this that it is necessary to oppose this deviance and return to the origins. The two new documents instead favor this deviance.

The picklock used is normative, above all through an instrument, the federations, that already exist but that now presents itself no longer as a choice but as an obligation. For justifying this line, *Cor orans* starts with the supposition that the monasteries are isolated among themselves and that they need to federate. The imaginary system presents itself (attention to the terminology, different from politics) under the forms of "federations of monasteries", "associations of monasteries", "confederation of monasteries", and "international commission". But, in all this, where is the Holy Ghost?

It is a mechanism that the author dismounts with only one, decisive affirmation:

> *The monasteries of contemplative female life have already overcome isolation because they are connected in Christ with God (the eschatological and vertical dimension) and between them (the temporal and horizontal dimension) for the action of the Holy Ghost.*

The Holy Ghost is in fact the soul of community life, even when the monasteries are only exteriorly connected between them. But this dynamic seems to escape the rulers, who, consequently, build the new normative building on a presumption that is simply wrong. And the result is disastrous: "The constitution VDq and the instruction *Cor orans* move the gravitational center of the link between the monasteries from the eschatological dimension to the temporal one".

In the presence of this "fatal move of the center of gravity" there is no norm that can survive, as the "Holy Ghost ceases to be the soul of the communion between the monasteries" and thus nothing can save them anymore, neither a new juridical ordinance nor a new organization.

It is true that *Vultum Dei quaerere* formally recognizes the juridical autonomy of the monasteries, but it is only an apparent confirmation. Once the center of gravity has been moved, the contemplative monastic life is injured to death. "Through the moving of the center of gravity from the eschatological dimension to the temporal one, the Holy Ghost has been eliminated as the soul of consecrated life." This occurs an irreparable rupture with Tradition: "the new revolutionary spirit has substituted the charisma of the Saintly founders, given to them by the Holy Ghost."

I know, dear reader: these are terrible words. But it is necessary to understand. We cannot think that, at the end, the problem regards only poor cloistered nuns dispersed through the world and without any real impact on our spiritual and religious life.

If we let the revolutionary spirit substitute the Holy Ghost, if we let this "fatal reversal" happen, if we allow that the adaptation to the world prevails over the search for holiness, we permit Satan, the enemy, to launch an unprecedented attack on God, "evidently not in Heaven, but in his work, that is humanity created in Christ, fallen in Adam but resurrected in Christ."

The author puts it in black and white: "The new revolutionary spirit is the principal informant of the instruction *Cor orans,* that contains 289 new practical norms. As a consequence, the instruction is ambiguous in a fundamental manner". And we know that ambiguity, that often feeds on bureaucratization and hyper normativism, is an unconfusable sign of the activity of the prince of darkness, he who divides.

The author points his attention also to the way in which the new norms claim to regulate the formation of the Nuns and concludes that, with all evidence, these norms have lost the point of view that in the formation of the Christian the supernatural and natural spirit constitute the principal part.

Cor orans, in fact, arrives at reversing the right order, stabilizing "an inverted scale of values: the primacy is occupied by human formation and no longer by spiritual formation, that is possible only through the work of the Holy Ghost".

Of course, *Cor orans* (thus the ambiguity) affirms that the formation, for consecrated life, "consists above all in identifying with Christ", but if the formation, de facto, is partial and inspired by the world, we are going in the contrary direction, and to this proposition the author is lapidary:

> *Animated by the new revolutionary spirit, the instruction Cor orans substitutes the supernatural and natural formation of the religious with a partial formation that practically leads to the secularization of their lives.*
>
> *The constitution VDq and the instruction Cor orans repeatedly praise the female contemplative life in the Church. But if the religious contemplatives of the different orders put on the uniform which belongs to the new revolutionary spirit, against the Holy Ghost, then they will cease to exist as such.*

Cultivating the primacy of God, the contemplative Nuns work with extraordinary efficiency for the salvation of souls, but if they accept the mundane and revolutionary spirit they would "enter into the way of perdition".

I do not want to anticipate here the conclusions to which the author will arrive at the end of his reflection. I will only say that he speaks of an "epochal crossroads" and that it is an "apocalyptic crossroads". In front of the crossroads one can find the contemplative Nuns, called to choose between God and the world, between loyalty to the charisms of their founders and the acceptance of the revolutionary spirit. But one can also find the Church and humanity, threatened by an extraordinary assault of Leviathan, the serpent, devious and twisted. "Only Jesus Christ crucified and resurrected (God one and Three) can defeat him, but he wants to do this through an extraordinary effusion of the Holy Ghost through the Immaculate Heart of the Woman clothed with the sun".

Never as today, thus, the Church and humanity have had such need of the contribution, with prayer and immolation, of the contemplative Nuns. "Their role is important as never before, because they are the principal praying rampart for the survival of the Church and humanity in the apocalyptic test".

He who has ears to understand….

LEGENDA

John Paul II, Apostolic Exhortation, Vita *consacrata* (1996) = John Paul II, **V.c.**

Francis, Apostolic Constitution, *Vultum Dei quaerere* on female contemplative life (2016) = Francis, **VDq.**

Congregation for the Institutes of Consecrated Life and Societies of Apostolic Life, Applicative Instruction of the Constitution VDq, "*Cor Orans*" (2018) = ***Cor orans***.

Instruction

The Second Vatican Council, as the start of the new, or second Pentecost, had identified in the Holy Ghost the central, global, supernatural and natural path for the renewal of consecrated life in the Church. Advancing on this path, the Conciliar Popes and the great Saints Paul VI and John Paul II worked for this renewal. The Congregation for the Institutes of Consecrated Life and the Society of Apostolic Life tried to follow in their footsteps. In this task were inserted the Apostolic Constitution VDq of Pope Francis and the Instruction *Cor orans* for its practical application, issued by the same Congregation. However, these two documents have caused great disturbance, perplexity and confusion in many female contemplative institutes. Are the two documents following the work of the last Council or presenting a novelty that deviates from the road that it traced?

On the basis of the teaching of the two saintly interpreters of the Council, who were Popes Paul VI and John Paul II, we will search the response to this question.

THE FIRST NEED OF THE CHURCH

Being one and identical in the head (Christ) and in his limbs, the Holy Ghost vivifies, unifies and moves all the Body (Mystical of the Church), so one of her actions can be compared by the Holy Fathers to the function that in the human body explains the principle of life, that of the soul (LG 7,7).

The Church lives of the Holy Ghost. The Church was really born, one can say, on the day of Pentecost. The first need of the Church is to always live the Pentecost.[1]

The Church is a continuation of the miracle of Pentecost. For this the first need of the Church is to live a perennial Pentecost of the Holy Ghost. It is the animator that "with the force of the Gospel rejuvenates the Church and continually renews it and conduces it to perfect union with

---

[1] Saint Paul VI, C. (Catechesis) *Perennial the presence and action of the Holy Ghost in the Church*, 12.10.1966. "The Church lives for the infusion of the Holy Ghost, an infusion that we call grace, that is a gift par excellence, charity, love of the Father, communicated to us in virtue of the redemption operated by Christ in the Holy Ghost. We remember the synthesis of Saint Augustine: "that which is the soul of the body of man is the Holy Ghost for the body of Christ, which is the Church". (*Sermon* 267)" (C. 16.10.1974).

her spouse" (LG 4), that is the Lord Jesus. In every epoch the evangelical renewal of the Church first and above all depends on the infusion of the Holy Ghost.

> *"The whole group of believers was united, heart and soul" (At 4, 32). In the Church the memory – maybe the nostalgia – of that primitive community has always remained, and deep-down religious communities have always tried to reproduce that ideal of communion in charity that has become the practical norm of life in common. (…) 'Only one heart and only one soul' does not mean uniformity, being monolithic or flattening, but profound communion in mutual comprehension and reciprocal respect. (…) The Council, an echo of the Acts of the Apostles, speaks of a "unity of the spirit" (PC 15). It deals with a unity which has its most profound origin in the Holy Ghost, which pours out charity in hearts (see Rom 5,5) and pushes diverse persons to aid each other in the path of perfection, installing and maintaining between them a climate of good agreement and cooperation. Just as it assures unity in all the Church, the Holy Ghost stabilizes it and causes it to endure in an even more intense way in the communities of consecrated life".*[2]

In the context of the continuation of the miracle of the first Pentecost the religious life was also born in the ancient Church, which realized the ideal of the first community in Jerusalem (see PC 15,1).

---

[2] Saint John Paul II, C. The common life in the evangelical light. 14.12.1994.

After the sunset of the ancient era, monasticism played a principle role in the formation of Christian Europe. The decline in the general level of the perennial Pentecost of the Church resulted in the oriental schism (1054) and afterwards the shipwreck of Catholic theology in nominalism (the XIV and XV centuries). From this shipwreck derived Protestantism (XVI century). From the same shipwreck the modern age developed as a new and great form of the city of Babylon that is opposed to the city of God, namely Jerusalem.[3] Its load bearing structure has becoming modern rationalist philosophy, from which derived atheist and anti-theist ideologies, and at the end the process of the globalization of the mystery of iniquity at a wide level.

In the last centuries the general level of the perennial Pentecost has fallen constantly. On the other and, the process of secularization of old Christian nations has augmented, and starting from the middle of the XIX century, their progressive great apostasy from Christ and his Gospel.

"Assuredly we have here a work of the Spirit, a gift of Pentecost. One must also recognize a prophetic intuition on the part of our

---

[3] According to the teaching of Saint Augustine, all the history of humanity is a march of the two opposing cities: of Jerusalem (the city of God) and of the city of Babylon (the city of the devil), see His celebrated work *The City of God*.

predecessor John XXIII, who envisaged a kind of new Pentecost as a fruit of the Council. (see Allocation 8.12.1962). We too have wished to place ourselves in the same perspective and in the same attitude of expectation. Not that Pentecost has ever ceased to be an actuality during the whole history of the Church, but so great are the needs and the perils of the present age, so vast the horizon of mankind drawn towards world coexistence and powerless to achieve it, that there is no salvation for it except in a new outpouring of the gift of God. Let him then come, the creating spirit, to renew the face of the earth!"[4]

Differently with the Tridentine Council, which focused on the visible and social dimension of the Church against some heresies of the Protestant reformation, the last Council "concentrated its attention on the spiritual,

---

[4] Saint Paul VI, Exhortation ap. *Gaudate in Domino*, 1975, n.7. The Council mentioned the Holy Ghost 258 times, see C. 23.5.1973. As the start of the second Pentecost, Vatican II was "in a special way an 'ecclesiological' Council: a Council on the theme of the Church. At the same time, the teaching of this Council is essentially 'pneumatological': it is permeated by the truth about the Holy Spirit as the soul of the Church. We can say that in its rich variety of teaching the Second Vatican Council contains all that 'the Spirit says to the Churches' (see Ap 2,29; 3,6.13.22) with regard to the present phase of the history of salvation" (John Paul II, Enc. *Dominum et vivificantem*, 1986, n 26).

mysterious and divine aspect of the Church, on the 'pneumatology' of the Church."⁵

The Second Vatican Council, as the start of the second Pentecost, reinforced the Pentecostal dimension of the Church. After the Council, the time of the sunset of the modern age, the Church, through a decisive elevation in the general level of the perennial Pentecost, entered into the new era and progressed towards "the unity of the human and Christian family" (Saint John XXIII, *Speech* 11.1.0.1962).

> *"In the Dogmatic Constitution on the Church, the Second Vatican Council declared that consecrated life, in its multiple forms, manifested "the infinite power of the Holy Ghost marvelously working in the Church" (LG 44,3). Similarly the Decree of the Council on the renewal of religious life underlined that it was the "impulse of the Holy Ghost" that gave origin both to the eremitical life and to the foundation of "religious families, which the Church gladly welcomed and approved by her authority" (PC 1,2).*⁶

The renewal of consecrated life in the Church is realized in the context of the second Pentecost. But not without the humble welcoming of the vivifying action of the Holy

---

⁵ Saint Paul VI, C. *The Holy Ghost: Fons vivus*, Ignis, Caritas, 16.5.1971.

⁶ Saint John Paul II, C. *The influence of the Holy Ghost on Consecrated Life*, 22.3.1995.

Ghost, the documents of the last Council would become for the reader the "letter" that kills (see 2 Cor 3,6): this goes also for the Dogmatic Constitution *Lumen gentium* and for the Decree *Perfectae caritatis*. Do they not maybe demonstrate this fact also the deviations that came out after the Council in the course of the actualization of the renewal of religious life?

> *"Among these, special attention needs to be given to two great documents of the Second Vatican Council: the Dogmatic Constitution on the Church Lumen Gentium and the Decree on the Renewal of Religious Life Perfectae Caritatis. The first of these sets the consecrated life within the ecclesiology of the People of God by virtue of the common call to holiness rooted in the consecration of Baptism. The second summons all consecrated persons to a fitting renewal in accordance with the changed conditions of the times. To guide such a renewal, the document proposes the following indispensable criteria: fidelity to Christ, to the Gospel, to one's own charism, to the Church, and to the men and women of our time" (see PC2) (Francis, VDq, 7).*

The reference of the Constitution Vdq7 to the text of the conciliar Decree PC 2 is important, because this number has a key significance for the right understanding of the Decree itself and for the realization of the Conciliar renewal regarding consecrated life. The above mentioned quadruple loyalty is however only realizable "under the impulse of the Holy Spirit" (PC2). It is surprising that VDq 7 does not mention this fact: this seems to be a significant omission in the Constitution.

The Constitution VDq mentions the Holy Ghost many times. After a prolonged and in-depth reflection on the document, an important question arises: is the Holy Ghost its soul? Is the Holy Ghost the soul of the renewal that this Constitution is introducing in female contemplative life? Does it take into account the fact that the first need of the contemplative religious is to live the second Pentecost?

A New Grand Ascension

The cloistered communities, posted as cities above mountains and lamps on the lampstands (cfr Mt 5, 14-15), even in the simplicity of their lives, visibly represent the goal towards which the whole ecclesiastical community is moving that "ardent in action and dedicated to contemplation", advances on the roads of time with its sight fixed on the future recapitulation of all in Christ, when the Church "will be revealed with him in glory" (cfr Col 3, 1-4)" (LG 9, 2), and Christ "will hand over the kingdom to God the Father, having abolished every principality, every ruling force and power (...) so that God may be in all" (1 Cor 15, 24.29).[7]

The city on the mountain of the Lord (of God one in three) is the supernatural and natural spiritual capital of the Church on earth: the "city of the spirit", because only supernatural and natural interior men erect above the level

---

[7] Saint John Paul II, V, c., 59. "Even in the simplicity of their life, cloistered communities, set like cities on a hilltop or lights on a lampstand (cf. *Mt* 5:14-15), visibly represent the goal towards which the entire community of the Church travels. 'Eager to act and yet devoted to contemplation', the Church advances down the paths of time with her eyes fixed on the future restoration of all things in Christ, when she will appear in glory" (Francis, Vdq, 2).

of exterior man, the exterior Church and the visible Church can enter it with the Holy Ghost.

> *"The economy of salvation is polarized towards the city of the spirit toward, of paradise tomorrow."*[8]

The level of the supernatural and natural city of the spirit is inconceivably elevated above the level of the visible Church and the sensible universe. The religious founders

---

[8] Saint Paul VI, *Easter Homily*, 6.4.1969. "If those who lived under the Old Law could sing of their earthly city: 'If I forget thee, O Jerusalem, let my right hand be forgotten; let my tongue cleave to my jaws if I do not remember thee, if I make not Jerusalem the beginning of my joy,' (Sal 136, 5-6), how much greater then should be the joy and exultation that should fill our hearts who dwell in a City built on the holy mountain of living and chosen stones, 'Jesus Christ himself being the chief cornerstone.' (Ed 2,20: 1 Pt 2, 4-5). For nothing more glorious, nothing nobler, nothing surely more honorable can be imagined than to belong to the One, Holy Catholic, Apostolic and Roman Church, in which we become members of One Body as venerable as it is unique; are guided by one supreme Head; are filled with one divine Spirit; are nourished during our earthly exile by one doctrine and one heavenly Bread, until at last we enter into the one, unending blessedness of heaven" (Pius XII, Enc. *Mystici corporis*, 1943). "The elect of the Holy Church enter into the city above the mountain, constituted in a culmination of virtue" (Saint Gregory the Great, *Homily on Ezechiele*, 1,7).

have chosen to scale the holy mountain of the Lord (of God one and three) and at the same time are advanced towards the celestial Jerusalem and towards the city of the spirit. They have walked with unceasing prayer and with docility towards the unsearchable ways of the Holy Ghost, with even an ever more intense exercise of faith, hope, charity and the supernatural and natural moral virtues. After the entrance of the 'city of the spirit', they are thus formed in it in perfect ranks according to Christ born, crucified, resurrected and ascended into heaven (in the second of God one and three), living in a heroic way according to his Gospel.

As citizens of the global city of the spirit, they have reached a certain supernatural and natural universality, that has gone beyond their time and all times. However, every one of them, "as alpine climbers of the spirit"[9] have opened their own proper characteristic pathway on the holy mountain of the Lord. He has become an example and a spiritual father for the mountaineers that are walking on his path: for his religious family.

According to the teaching of the Council, the

> *"renewal of the religious life includes both the constant return to the sources of all Christian life and to the original spirit of the institutes" (PC2): as it is, and this goes for every essential form of life; but then the Decree proceeds:... and entails 'their adaptation to the changed*

---

[9] Saint Paul VI, *Speech*, 26.9.1970.

conditions of our time' (PC2). The renewal thus consists in two programmatic parts, that we can define as the restoration of proper identity, (...) we can also say interior renewal"; the other programmatic point instead regards exterior and contingent renewal".[10]

The Second Vatican Council renewed, in an essential continuation with Sacred Tradition and Holy Scripture and with an integration of the positive part of modern culture, the Church as the city above the mountain: this is the evangelical "renewal" of the Church. Through the universal call to holiness (see LG 39-42), the Council promoted a new ascension of all states of the pilgrim people on the holy mountain of the Lord (of God one and three) and thus towards the celestial Jerusalem and towards the city on the mountain. All the persons consecrated to God who live according to the three evangelical counsels and "closely" follow the Lord, are called to walk at the head of this new divine (supernatural) and human (natural) ascent. With the

---

[10] Saint Paul VI, C. 13.8.1975. "The Council has determined the fundamental criteria that needs to guide the religious: the 'renewal of the religious life includes both the constant return to the sources of all Christian life and to the original spirit of the institutes'" (PC 2) see *Allocation to the Passionist religious*, 22.12.1971. "The renewal of the religious life comes from the primitive spirit, wisely adopts itself to the conditions and necessities of the times, and affronts the future with superior trust and unexhausted breath (see PC 2)" (*Speech* 23.12.1974).

spirit they must ascend to the city on the mountain, where their founders lived. The Conciliar renewal of religious life is achieved through this decisive ascent in holiness.[11]

With supernatural and natural interior ascension, the members of religious orders have a "constant return to the sources of all Christian life and to the original spirit of the institutes" (PC 2). In this way they restore their identity and eliminate imperfections, the superfluous and antique things that in the course of centuries were deposited in their orders. From this essential supernatural and natural renewal derives an adaption to the mutated conditions of the times, and with it also an exterior renewal. The first renewal is first and above all the work of the Holy Ghost, and the consequent adaptation is also its work, although much less important.

> *"It should be constantly kept in mind, therefore, that even the best adjustments made in accordance with the needs of our age will be ineffectual unless they are animated by a renewal of spirit. This must take precedence over even the active ministry"* (PC 2 e).

---

[11] "To tend towards holiness: this is in summary the program of every consecrated life, particularly in the perspective of its renewal" (Saint John Paul II, V.c., 93). "Today a renewed commitment to holiness by consecrated persons is more necessary than ever" (V. c. 39).

> *"Monasticism and the contemplative life are a constant reminder that the primacy of God gives full meaning and joy to human lives, because men and women are made for God, and their hearts are restless until they rest in him".*[12]

The Holy Ghost has given charisma to the founders, and thus it stands at the origin of religious communities.

> *"In religious life in fact, and in any consecrated life there is a sovereign and decisive action of the Holy Ghost. (...) It is he the guide of consecrated souls on the road of perfection. (...) The Holy Ghost has always grown the harmony of congregated persons and helped them*

---

[12] Saint John Paul II, V. c., 27. "The religious state clearly manifests that the Kingdom of God and its needs, in a very special way, are raised above all earthly considerations. Finally it clearly shows all men both the unsurpassed breadth of the strength of Christ the King and the infinite power of the Holy Spirit marvelously working in the Church." (LG 44, 3). "In other words life according to the evangelical counsels manifests the supernatural and transcendent majesty of God one and three, and in particular the height of the plan of the Father. (...) It reveals the attractive force of Christ, word incarnate; (...) it is a sign of the transforming power of the Holy Ghost which pours out on all souls the gifts of eternal love " (C. *The consecrated life sign and testimony of the reign of Christ*, 9.2.1995).

develop a common life animated by charity, according to the particular orientation of the charisma of the founder".[13]

"*It is necessary that you be the imitators of Christ, like the ecumenical assembly has exhorted to all religious* (see PC 2 a). *It is necessary to put on Christ all days, that is the principle and the end and the constitution (compages) of all your conduct (conversationis), of both singles and of your communities*".[14]

All members of religious orders ascend behind Christ on Mount Tabor (the mountain of the Transfiguration) and on Mount Calvary (the mountain of the crucifixion and resurrection) and thus in Christ and for Christ gradually enter into the reign and life of the Father and the Son and the Holy Ghost (see John Paul II, V. c., 14-21; 23-24; 40). In virtue of the descent of the Holy Ghost (of Christ in the Holy Ghost) they daily put on Christ born, crucified, resurrected and ascended into Heaven and take off the residues of the old man (sinful). The magnificent ascension

---

[13] Saint John Paul II, C. The influence of the Holy Ghost in consecrated life, 22.3.1995.

[14] Saint Paul VI, Allocation to the general chapter of the Redemptorists, 6.10.1973. The consecrated persons are bearers of the Cross *(stauropborsa)* and of the Spirit *(pneumatopboros)* (see John Paul II, V. C., 6), as they are taken to Christ crucified and resurrected with the power of the Holy Ghost.

is the continuation of the Pentecostal miracle in their lives, as it was with their founders.

Their transformation in Christ is a "new creation" (2 Cor 5,17), namely a process of their divinization and humanization: an ineffably excellent work of the Holy Trinity that surpasses the creation of the visible sky and earth. However, it demands the personal cooperation of all members of religious institutes. Without pause they need to be docile to the incomprehensible paths of the Holy Ghost, develop in the virtuous supernatural and natural life, in prayer, in contemplation and in action. This goes in particular for all contemplative religious.

> *"The renewal did not have and does not have any other objective than that of presenting to the world, in as close an image as possible, the very figure of the Lord, 'in contemplation on the mountain, in his proclamation of the kingdom of God to the multitudes (…)' (LG 46). Welcome is this renewal thus, which is inspired by such a high model and aims at such a noble goal! But if, on the other hand, the wind of dissatisfaction causes surrender to the mundane mentality, to the following of ephemeral and changeable trends and behaviors, to camouflaging with the world in its forms, without discernment and without criteria, then, you should be convinced, the result would also be really deplorable: 'You are salt for the earth. But if salt loses its taste, what can make it salty again? It is good for nothing, and can only be thrown out to be trampled under people's feet' (Mt 5, 13).*

> *The un, likewise for the priest and the religious, even if in another prospective, are in front of a terrible dilemma: or Saints, totally without compromise, to reach their full dimension, or reduce themselves to jokes, to caricatures, to being botched, and, let us say, aborted. The dangers of secularization are evident, in all reflexes, and particularly for poverty, when one searches for an economic autonomy that is in contrast with the spirit of renunciation of the Gospel and religious life".*[15]

Through the elevation of the level of supernatural and natural dynamic of the virtues one achieves a new great ascension of consecrated life on the holy mountain of the Lord (God one and three), that is its renewal. Realizing this elevation is however possible only with a docile welcome of the growing effusion of the Holy Ghost with its seven gifts. Therefore, it is absolutely necessary to humbly implore this effusion through a persevering prayer with the Virgin Mother of God and Spouse of the Holy Ghost, who is also the Mother of the order of grace (see LG 60-62) and Mother of the Church in the Cenacle of Pentecost; implore her particularly with the humble recitation of the holy Rosary.[16] When the ascent reaches the city on the mountain

---

[15] Saint Paul VI, *Speech to the 550 religious superiors of all nations*, 22.11.1969.

[16] "Spiritually the event of Pentecost does not belong only to the past: the Church is always in the Upper Room that she bears in her heart. The Church perseveres in preserves, like the Apostles together with Mary, the Mother of Christ" (Saint John

and stabilizes there with a perfect exercise of the virtues, then one can also ensure a correct adaptation of the religious institutes to the mutated conditions of the times.

The Church is "present in the world and yet not at home in it" (SC 2). "The Church, "like a stranger in a foreign land, presses forward amid the persecutions of the world and the consolations of God, announcing the cross and death of the Lord until he comes (see 1 Cor 11, 26)" (LG 8, 5). The relationship of the pilgrim Church with the world in evolution excludes two opposite attitudes: immobilism and relativism. In practice it is difficult to find an equilibrium and a synthesis between them.[17]

Paul II, Enc. *Dominum et vivificantem*, 66). On the prayer of the Rosary, see Saint Paul VI, Ap Exhortation., *Marialis cultus*, 1974, n. 40-55; John Paul II, Ap Letter., *Rosarium Virginis Mariae*, 2002.

[17] See Saint Paul VI, C. 13.5.1970. "It is necessary to find the line of complementarity (between two attitudes): we have to be good in maintaining that which for us is the reason of life and source of light and of energy, the 'deposit' we said, the faithful coherence with Tradition, from where comes the Christian life in its irreplaceable and immutable elements; and we have to be equally good in modeling the contingent forms of Christian ecclesial customs to the necessities of our modern cohabitation and even more of our mission according to the changing of circumstances, of places, and of times" (the same C.). The Pope affirms that relativism is today a particularly tempting attitude. Many after the Council have welcomed it, maybe without

The royal path of the Church does not deviate to the right or to the left (see Nm 4, 17; Dt 5, 32-33): it is the central global way of equilibrium and synthesis between two contrary attitudes. The Church walks in every century on this difficult path of Christian virtues, which is that of ascension, by the work of the Holy Ghost, of the mountain of Christ crucified and resurrected. Under the motion of the Holy Ghost, this difficult path was walked in their times by the saintly founders of the religious orders with the heroic exercise of the virtues.

After the Council the religious orders that have declined from the charisma of their holy founders have regressed. In the measure in which they have given in to the pressure of a contrary wind (see Gv 6, 14-18), they have neglected the life of the spirit of the Second Pentecost, and with that supernatural and natural renewal. While they have fallen from the holy mountain of the crucified and resurrected Lord, they have come closer in a disordered way to the contemporary world: surrendering to the mundane mentality, they have promoted an exaggerated adaptation to the mutated conditions of the times. In this way, the vortex of secularization has affected them in a more or less big measure: they entered into crisis and vocations have fallen or stopped. Numerous religious orders have suffered heavy

---

realizing it, and have become subjects of the 'dictatorship of relativism' (Benedict XVI).

losses, in part visible and in part invisible, with the secularization of a part of their members. Has the cortex of secularization not penetrated in many great orders, noted for their glorious histories? And is this fact not perhaps the most tragic result of the false renewal after the Council?

THE HOLY GHOST, SOUL OF COMMUNITARIAN LIFE

Present in the context of the second Pentecost is the renewal of consecrated life, which postulates a new great ascension of all religious on the holy mountain of the Lord (God one and three). Through this ascension the spirits, through the work of the Holy Ghost, come closer to one another, and in this way the federations of the same religious family can organically grow together, without the monasteries losing their just autonomies; new unions of the same religious family can grow in an organic manner, "if they can be considered as belonging to the same religious family" (PC 22); or even more ample associations (see PC 23: John Paul II, V.c., 59).

> *"Federation of monasteries means a structure of communion among some autonomous monasteries of the same Institute, erected by the Holy See that approves the Statutes, so that in sharing the same charism, the federated monasteries overcome isolation and promote regular observance and contemplative life"* (*Cor orans*, 7; see Norm 86 which recalls VDq, 28-30).

The instruction *Cor orans* starts with the presumption that the monasteries are isolated among themselves. To overcome this isolation *Cor orans* emanated new norms which instituted the Federation of monasteries, the

Association of monasteries, the Conference of monasteries, the Confederation of monasteries, the International Commission and the female monastic Congregation (norms 7-14) and determined their activities in a detailed way (norms 86-115). It seems that the instruction refers according to the "letter", somehow, to the doctrine of the Council (see PC 22-23). However, does it refer also to the "spirit"?

The instruction *Cor orans* translated into the new practical norms the spirit of the Constitution VDq, 28-30 and article 9 at the end of the Constitution.

"Soul of the Mystical Body, the Holy Ghost is the soul of every communitarian life"[18].

The monasteries of female consecrated life have already overcome isolation, because they are connected in Christ with God (the vertical eschatological dimension) and between them (the horizontal temporal dimension) through the action of the Holy Ghost. The Holy Ghost is the soul of their communitarian life even when they are not exteriorly connected with each other. The female contemplative institutions are rooted in the life of the three divine persons (in their infinite and eternal penetration, that is in their mutual interpretation and embrace), and thus live

---

[18] Saint John Paul II, C. *The influence of the Holy Ghost in consecrated life*, 22.3.1995.

between them in a more or less profound communion. Is there any greater link and communion between them than that stabilized by the Holy Ghost, which is their soul? The presumption that the monasteries are isolated between them is thus wrong.

The Constitution VDq and the Instruction *Cor orans* move the gravitational center of the link between the monasteries from the eschatological dimension to the temporal one. But with this fatal moving of the center of gravity, the Holy Ghost ceases to be the soul of communion between the monasteries. Without him, they will slide into spiritual isolation and will succumb to the "disease of self-absorption" (Francis, VDq, 29).

No human structure of communion will save them from this deadly sickness of egoism. Not even the new juridical ordinance and the new organization introduced by the Constitution VDq and the Instruction *Cor orans* will save them.

The Constitution VDq (see N. 28 and article 8, paragraph 1) and equally the Instruction *Cor orans* (see Norms 15-18) recognize the juridical autonomy of the monasteries. But with the decline in spiritual isolation, the monasteries will also lose their juridical autonomy, which they have had throughout the course of their histories. Thus, in both documents the confirmation of their juridical autonomy is only apparent. A new juridical ordinance, in harmony with the new center of gravity, has taken its place.

The Renewal is not a Revolution

Maybe you did not think that the Council would also have dealt with religious life, and would also have entered your inviolate cloisters to dictate laws. You should not think, dear daughters, that the Council is a type of overwhelming tornado, almost a revolution, that subverts ideas and mores and that permits unthinkable and thoughtless novelties. No, the Council is a renewal, not a revolution; and you can see this as the first criteria that guides its intervention in your sector, more in that of loyalty to origins than an abandonment of genuine traditions. The Council said that the: "renewal of the religious life includes both the constant return to the sources of all Christian life and to the original spirit of the institutes" (PC 2).

> *It is thus not a tearing up of origins, but a return to the origins of the very institutes, to draw the authentic vital sap, not exhausted by years of the changes of history, that can and must even today produce novelties. Life is a perennial novelty. In your case, it must be a novelty of conscience, a novelty of virtue, a novelty of works, a novelty of love.*[19]

---

[19] Saint Paul VI, speech to the Abbesses of Benedictine monasteries in Italy, 28.10.1966. The Council prescribes: "Think again to the origins above all. This is the first renewal: looking back to go ahead in the right direction. The path is marked at its

Through the moving of the center of gravity from the eschatological dimension to the temporal one, the Holy Ghost as the soul of consecrated life has been eliminated. At the same time a rupture with the teaching of the last universal Council on the renewal of religious life has taken place, and with that also with Sacred Tradition. A profound revolution has taken place. The new revolutionary spirit has substituted the charisma of the founders, given to them by the Holy Ghost.

This revolutionary spirit overturns the first and fundamental Conciliar criteria on the renewal of religious life. As a consequence, it removes the supernatural and natural ascension of the institutes of female contemplative life on the holy mountain of the Lord (of God one and three) and thus towards the celestial Jerusalem and towards the city of the spirit. Moreover, it empties their dynamic of supernatural and natural virtues and at the same time their spiritual renewal. In effect, after the fatal overturn, an adaption to the mutated conditions of the times has

---

departure. The tree lives of its roots. And there is no doubt that your most vital root is the teaching of St Teresa (of Avila): this goes principally for the Carmelite Nuns, but in its fundamental cannons and in its spirit this goes also for you; every opportune adaptation must not contradict or deform the characteristic religious physiognomy that this reforming founder marked on Carmel" (*Allocation to the members of the general chapter of the barefooted Carmelites*, 22.6.1967).

prevailed. Substituting natural and supernatural renewal, this adaption affirms, in effect, the primacy of exterior renewal, namely of the casing.

The contemplative religious should, on the footsteps of their saintly founders, ascend with a new rush on the salvific mountain of the crucified and resurrected Christ and towards the city of the spirit. However, following the new fundamental orientation, in which an adaptation to the mutated conditions of the times prevails, they will leave this mountain behind their backs and will proceed in a contrary direction: they will thus enter into the vortex of a subtle and profound secularization. An incredibly violent tornado threatens to rip away 37,970 elected fruit trees of diverse species (the contemplative religious) together with their roots and to knock them down.

> *"The Congregation for Institutes of Consecrated Life and Societies of Apostolic Life will issue, in accordance with the spirit and the norms of the present Apostolic Constitution, a new Instruction concerning the matters dealt with in No. 12"* (Francis, VDq, article 14, paragraph 1).

The new revolutionary spirit is the principle informant of the instruction *Cor orans*, which contains 289 new practical norms. As a consequence, the instruction is ambiguous in a fundamental manner. Under its positive mantle it hides and introduces in practice this spirit in female contemplative life. To realize this substantial transformation, the instruction has fabricated a spiritual uniform (the form of life), that the contemplative religious of the diverse families must wear by the first of April 2019. With this "coating" they will de facto in their hearts undress their proper charismatic uniform (the form of life): they will cease to be religious of their own order and religious in general. Breaking the link with Sacred Tradition, they will subjectively put themselves with pride above the charisma of their saintly founders, and in this way also above the Holy Ghost.

A NEW FORMATION

Our Christian life must be modeled and inspired by the great novelty that is grace, that is the action of the Holy Ghost in souls associated with the life of Christ. It is this essential and charismatic aspect of the "new law", that of the Gospels that flourishes in the Church. (...) "The new law is chiefly the grace of the Holy Ghost, inscribed on the hearts of the faithful... The new law (...) is the grace of the Holy Ghost" (Saint Thomas Aquinas, S. th., I-II q. 106, a. 1 and 2).

Really think of what novelty, what liberty, what interiority, what spirituality defines the authenticity of the Christian life. First, and in a certain sense, our only duty: living in the grace of God; that is then resolvable in the biggest and summarizing precept of Christ: living in the love of God and of your neighbor (see Mt 22, 37).[20]

---

[20] Saint Paul VI, C. *The criteria of authenticity in the Christian life*, 23.6.1971. "In what way does the Holy Ghost constitute the new and eternal alliance? Removing sin and re-pouring the love of God into the heart of man: 'the law of the spirit which gives life in Christ Jesus has set you free from the law of sin and death' (Rom 8,2). '(...) Saint Thomas Aquinas sharply affirmed that the Holy Ghost itself is the new alliance, operating in us love, the fullness of the law (see Comment 2 Cor 3, 6). '(...) From the

Have all the saintly founders of female contemplative orders not perhaps all acted according to the "law of the spirit which gives life in Christ Jesus"? Did the Holy Ghost not write the law of the new alliance on their hearts? And was this not their great novelty and liberty? If we think to the life of Saint Clare, who was attracted by the example of Saint Francis of Assisi, who in an extraordinarily heroic way formed and acted according to the law of the Gospel![21] Do the constitutions of their orders not express this fact? And were they not already renewed after the last Council?

The Constitution VDq stabilizes a new form of formation for the contemplative religious (see N. 13-15 and article 3 with paragraphs 1-7).

The instruction *Cor orans* with the norms 219-289 stabilizes as obligatory, for all institutes of female

---

fact that the Holy Ghost is the 'new alliance', derives that the work of the third person of the Holy Trinity consists in rendering present the resurrected Lord and with him God the Father. The spirit in fact exercises its salvific action rendering immediate the presence of God. In this consists the new and eternal alliance: God has already made himself accessible to every one of us" (Saint John Paul II, C, 17.6.1998).

[21] "Thus the Council rightly insists on the obligation of religious to be faithful to the spirit of their founders, to their evangelical intentions and to the example of their sanctity" (Saint Paul VI, Ap Exhortation., *Evangelica testificatio*, 1971, n. 11). See John Paul II, V. c., 48.

contemplative life, the new form of initial and permanent formation. This belongs to the new uniform that the contemplative religious have to wear. However, does the new formation consist primarily in the grace of the Holy Ghost? Is it in harmony with the evangelical law?

> *"This education must blend its elements together harmoniously so that an integrated life on the part of the religious concerned results. Religious should strive during the whole course of their lives to perfect the culture they have received in matters spiritual and in arts and sciences"* (PC 18, 2-3).
>
> *"Formation in contemplative monastic life is based on a personal encounter with the Lord. It begins with the call of God and the decision of each one to follow, according to her own charism, the footsteps of Christ, as His disciple, under the action of the Holy Spirit"* (Cor orans, 332: see Norm 224).

This norm is correct. However a contradiction emerges if we compare it with the following norm:

> *"Formation for the contemplative monastic life must be integral, that is, taking the person as a whole into account so that she develops her own psychic, moral, affective, and intellectual gifts harmoniously and becomes actively involved in community life. None of these dimensions of the person must remain excluded from the scope of either initial or ongoing formation"* (Cor orans, 225).

The Council put in the first place spiritual (formation) knowledge (see PC 18,), because without it no "spiritual renewal" (PC 2 e) can exist. In the integral formation of religious life spiritual formation is never missing (see John Paul II, V.c., 60; 65). The instruction *Cor orans* left out the spiritual formation of the contemplative religious. Consequently its "integral formation" is necessarily partial. The instruction has lost sight of the fact that in the constitution of the Christian the supernatural and natural spirit is the principal and also most precious part, as the divine redeemer taught in the last instant of his life: "but Jesus cried out again in a loud voice, and gave up his spirit" (Mt 27, 50; see Gv 19, 30). The instruction also overturns, in effect, the right order and stabilizes an inverted order of values: the primacy is occupied by human formation and no longer by spiritual formation, which is possibly only through the work of the Holy Ghost.

"The economy of the Gospel is all turned towards waking and expanding the interior reign of the spirit".[22]

---

[22] Saint Paul VI, *Speech* 19.10.1970. "The Council, in postulating with strong words the necessary renewal (of the religious life), put above all the accent on the primacy of the spiritual life, without which even any merely human splendid gift and talented capacity, even any voluntarily effort, cannot but be reduced to a ringing harpsichord, a resonant but empty bronze: 'let those who make profession of the evangelical counsels seek and love above all else God who has first loved us (see 1 John 4:10) and let them strive to foster in all circumstances a life

> *"The spiritual life, intended as life in Christ, life according to the spirit, is configured as an itinerary of increasing loyalty, in which the consecrated person is guided by the spirit and by himself configured in Christ, in full communion of love and of service in the Church. (…) The spiritual life thus must be at the first place in the program of the families of consecrated life, in a way that any institute and any community can present themselves as schools of real evangelical spirituality".*[23]

---

hidden with Christ in God (see Col. 3:3). This love of God both excites and energizes that love of one's neighbor which contributes to the salvation of the world and the building up of the Church. This love, in addition, quickens and directs the actual practice of the evangelical counsels. Drawing therefore upon the authentic sources of Christian spirituality, members of religious communities should resolutely cultivate both the spirit and practice of prayer.' (PC 6). (*Speech to the members of the General Chapters of some religious orders*, 14.9.1968).

[23] Saint John Paul II, V. c., 93. "God the Father, through the unceasing gift of Christ and the Spirit, is the educator *par excellence* of those who consecrate themselves to him" (V.c., 66). "The Spirit who awakens the desire to respond fully; it is he who guides the growth of this desire, helping it to mature into a positive response and sustaining it as it is faithfully translated into action; it is he who shapes and moulds the hearts of those who are called, configuring them to Christ, the chaste, poor and obedient one" (V.c. 19). "Life in the Spirit is clearly of primary importance. Living in the Spirit, consecrated persons discover their own identity and find profound peace" (V.c., 71). "The first missionary duty of consecrated persons is to themselves,

The initial and permanent formation of the religious contemplatives, those natural and supernatural women, belong to their ascension on the holy mountain of the Lord (God one and three). In them not only does God the Father act, but also the Holy Ghost in Christ and through Christ. Through a sovereign and decisive action of the Holy Ghost, the spirits of the religious "wake up and expand", as they are gradually entering into the intimate life of God infinite and eternal. At the same time a supernatural and natural communion grows among them. The formation is integral, because it involves all the other supernatural and natural dimensions of the religious. It develops in harmony with the authentic evangelical economy and is a school of real evangelical spirituality.

"Under the action of the Holy Spirit, both candidates and nuns are the main protagonists of their formation and responsible for accepting and internalizing all the values of the monastic life." (*Cor orans*, 227). This norm is correct, if it refers to the integral formation of the religious contemplatives, it is wrong, if it refers to their partial formation. The Holy Ghost, which guides towards the whole truth (see Gv 16,13) is not in fact the teacher of a

---

and they fulfil it by opening their hearts to the promptings of the Spirit of Christ." (V.c., 25). "Consecrated persons should remember that before all else they must be expert guides in the spiritual life, and in this perspective they should cultivate "the most precious gift: the spirit"." (V.c., 55).

partial formation, which is contrary to the economy of the Gospel and evolves in an opposite direction. The teacher and guide of this formation is a spirit which is contrary to the spirit of truth and of love.

> *"While the acquisition of knowledge remains important, formation in the consecrated life, and particularly in contemplative monastic life, consists above all in identifying with Christ"* (Cor orans, 222).

This norm is correct. However such a formation can be realized only through the action of the Holy Ghost, it being a continuation of the Pentecostal miracle. A partial formation does not conduce the contemplative religious to mystical identification with Christ, as it advances in a contrary direction. Animated by the new revolutionary spirit, the instruction *Cor orans* substitutes the supernatural and natural formation of the religious with a partial formation, that practically conduces to the secularization of their lives.

THE GREATEST STRUGGLE OF THE DRAGON

> *"That day Yahweh will punish, with his unyielding sword, massive and strong, Leviathan the fleeing serpent, Leviathan the coiling serpent; he will kill that dragon that lives in the sea" (Is 27, 1). According to the Hebrew tradition the devil, that is the accuser (a Greek word), is called satan, that is the adversary. (...) He is the sea monster of which the book of Job narrates in a mysterious way its capture by Christ (see Jb 3, 8). (...) And it is written in a Psalm: 'Then there is the sea, with its vast expanses teeming with countless creatures, creatures both great and small; there ships pass to and fro, and Leviathan whom you made to sport with'" (Ps 104, 35, 36).*[24]

The apparitions of the Virgin Mary in Fatima (1917) were a great sign from Heaven of the start of the actualization of the last book of Holy Scripture: the Apocalypse. The Holy Father John Paul II spoke in Fatima of the great struggle of the dragon in history with humanity, and in a certain sense also with the Church. Leviathan has advanced and advances with success in his struggle, adopting first and above all the method of a "half temptation of pride" (John Paul II) and with this also a temptation of "omniscient pride" (Benedict XVI).

---

[24] Saint Jerome, *Commentary on Isaiah*, VIII, 30. See John Paul II, Enc. *Dominum et vivificantem*, 37-38.

In the last period of his Pontificate, Saint John Paul II explained the book of the Apocalypse, that the "end of times" is being realized on the Earth of men. The progress of events in humanity and in the Church testify to this.

After the Second World War a very profound process of the globalization of the mystery of iniquity has been progressing, which tends to a homologation of all religions and all cultures. The curve of pride advances in the world towards its culmination (the maximum), provoking the refusal of the love of God one and triune: this process brings the threat of the auto destruction of humanity (see GS 37, 1).[25]

Leviathan has attacked God one and triune has never before in history, evidently not in Heaven, but instead in his work, which is humanity created in Christ, fallen in Adam but redeemed b Christ. The Ecumenical Second Vatican Council set itself against this process with the realization, at its level, of the victorious design of God regarding the great recapitulation of all of creation in Christ (God one and three) (see GS 45). This will come with the extraordinary fullness of the second Pentecost.

---

[25] "Humanity now has instruments of unprecedented power: we can turn this world into a garden, or reduce it to a pile of rubble. (…) Today as never before in the past, humanity stands at a crossroads. And once again, O Virgin Most Holy, salvation lies fully and uniquely in Jesus, your Son." (Saint John Paul II, *Jubilee of Bishops, Act of Entrustment to Mary*, 8.10.2000).

"The Sacred Council promotes the spirit of evangelical renewal of the Church in Christ (see OT, in the end and at the introduction). This process is realizable only through the work of the Holy Ghost, namely as a new Pentecost. Therefore the Council has enormously magnified the great mystery of the animation of the Church through the virtue of the Holy Ghost".[26]

"That the Council has received and still has as its general end a renewal of all the Church (see OT, introduction and conclusion.; LG 4; 15; UR, 6; etc.) and of all human activity, also in the profane sphere (GS 43), is the truth that transpires from every document and from the very fact of the Council. (...)

It is to be noted that the interest for the renewal was welcomed by many turned towards the exterior and impersonal transformation of the ecclesiastical edifice and to the acceptation of the forms and of the spirit of the protestant reformation, instead of that first and foremost moral, personal and interior renewal that the Council wanted; that which must rejuvenate the Church in the conscience of her mystery, of her adhesion to Christ, of her animation through the virtue of the Holy Ghost".[27]

---

[26] See Saint Paul VI, C. 26.3.1969.

[27] Saint Paul VI, C. *Principal and personal the renewal stabilized by the Council*, 15.1.1969. "The principal renewal, we remember well, is interior, is personal (see LG 7-15; UR 4-7-8). Saint Paul recommended: 'your mind was to be renewed in spirit' (Ef 4, 23): this is the true, the first, and our Christian novelty" (C. *Sine ruga et sine macula*, 2.7.1969).

Leviathan has launched, after the Council, the greatest, most profound and subtle attack in history against God one and triune, evidently not in Heaven, but in the Catholic Church, where he lives. Obscuring the role of the "Woman clothed with the sun" (Ap 12, 1), the "smoke of Satan" (Paul VI) has created an incredible confusion "of traffic", first and above all at the level of the clergy (cfr Ap 12, 4), whence it was diffused in other ranks of the itinerant Catholic people. Leviathan, the wriggling and torturous serpent (see Is 27, 1), with an extraordinary activity of his satellite system was able to spread errors and heresies in an ambiguous way as never seen before to conduce the Church little by little to a general apostasy from the Gospel and thus finally triumph over Jesus of Nazareth (God one and triune).

The supernatural and natural spirit of the Council, which is that of the new Pentecost, was substituted to an inconceivably profound level, and thus occulted, by the spirit of a false renewal: by the spirit of the Protestant reformation, above all by the fundamental spirit of the modern world. This has provoked an ever more profound and vast process of secularization, with which apostasy from Christ and from the Church has spread. And on the other side, a false Christ and a false Church has been formed. The process has augmented over decades and decades and in our time the culmination (the maximum) has truly advanced.

At an Epochal Crossroads

"The Church and the world have need as never before that the prodigy of Pentecost continues in history".[28]

The earth of men has come to an apocalyptic crossroads: the survival of the Church and of humanity is threatened by an extraordinary attack of Leviathan and of his satellite system. Only Christ crucified and resurrected (God one and three) can defeat him, but he wants to do this through an extraordinary effusion of the Holy Ghost through the Immaculate Heart of the Woman clothed with the sun. Therefore, the renewal of the face of the earth will come with an extraordinary intervention of the omnipotent creative spirit, thus with a universal Pentecost. Otherwise there is no salvation, as Pope Paul VI had already affirmed.

---

[28] Saint Paul VI, *Speech* 19.5.1975. The mystery of the Church and of her life is "the Holy Ghost, animator and sanctifier of the Church, her divine breath, the wind of her sails, her principal unifier, her surging interior of light and of force, her support and her consolation, her pledge and prelude of blessed and eternal life (see LG 5). (…) The Church has need of its perennial Pentecost. (…) She has need of the Holy Ghost" (C. *The Holy Ghost animator and sanctifier of the Church*, 29.11.1972). "Among all of them, our first devotion must be to the Holy Ghost" (C. 17.6.1967).

The Church and humanity have need more than over of the Holy Ghost. Thus, they have need more than ever of the contribution of the prayer and of the immolation of the contemplative religious, because they humbly implore the gift of the Most High. Their role is more important than ever, because they are the principal praying rampart of the survival of the Church and of humanity in the apocalyptic test.

> *"The Church is the continuation of Christ in time. We cannot break away from her, like a branch, that wants to explode in the new flowers of spring, it cannot break away from the plant, from the root, from which it receives its vitality. This is one of the capital points of the contemporary history of Christianity: it is a decisive point: or faithful and fertile adhesion with the authentic and authoritative tradition of the Church, or the mortal cut away from her".*[29]

---

[29] Saint Paul VI, C. *Renewal in loyalty: the post-conciliar program*, 12.8.1970. "Novelty" is a word with double meaning: in the positive aspect it expresses an uninterrupted fidelity to the essential doctrine of the Church, in its negative expression however, a rupture with Sacred Tradition, see C. 28.10.1970. The immutability of the deposit of faith, that the Church conserves, "is born from the same roots of the Church that draws their sap in the past, through Christ, until they arrive to the same sense of God. (…) There is no contraposition at all between life and immutability: to the contrary, it is life that assures the essential immutability of a living being" (*Allocation to the College of Cardinals*, 20.12.1976).

After the Ecumenical Second Vatican Council, the itinerant Catholic people found themselves at an epochal crossroads: a part of them are proceeding on the way of the second Pentecost remaining loyal to Sacred Tradition, and thus with Christ; the other is giving up to the spirit of secularization and of the rupture with Sacred Tradition, and thus with Christ. In the first direction the people are realizing evangelical renewal in the Church, however in the second direction "a false secularizing renewal that is in reality not renewal but destroys".[30] The gap and the contraposition between the two directions have augmented over the years, and in our time have arrived at the last phase.

Only by augmenting devotion to the Holy Ghost, prayer in the Cenacle with its spouse, the Virgin Mary, and the life of consecration to her Immaculate Heart, can the people receive a victorious aid from up high: they can thus remain loyal to Jesus Christ, overcome all the obstacles on the way and the extraordinary attacks of Leviathan and his satellite system.

"The religious institutes of contemplative and active life have up to now had a very important role in the evangelization of the world. (...) With their prayers, penances and tribulations the institutes of consecrated life have had the maximum importance in the conversion of souls, because it is God who, receiving prayers, sends workers into his masses (see Mt 9, 38), opens the souls of non-Christians to hear the Gospel (see At 16,

---

[30] Saint John Paul II, *Speech*, 22.6.1984.

14) and fecunds in their hearts the word of salvation (see 1 Cor 2, 7) (AG 40, 1. 2; see PC 7).

> *In the constituted body of the Church there are different organs and functions. The contemplatives represent the highest and most difficult function: to think to the Lord, to be silent, to pray, to adore, to rejoice in renunciation and in penance".*[31]

The task of the ecclesiastical hierarchy is to aid the religious institutes with its authority, "in order that these same institutes may grow and flourish according to the spirit of the founders." (LG 35, 1).

The Constitution VDq and the Instruction *Cor orans* repeatedly praise female contemplative life in the Church. But if the contemplative religious of the different orders put on the uniform that belongs to the new revolutionary spirit, contrary to the Holy Ghost, then they will cease to exist as such.

"The consecrated life is important precisely in its being *unbounded generosity and love*, and this all the more so in a world which risks being suffocated in the whirlpool of the ephemeral" (Saint John Paul II, V.c., 105). The religious contemplatives, that should have been the maximum counterweight in the Church to the gigantic vortex of the modern world, will sink in it and will submit to the new

---

[31] Saint Paul VI, *Allocation to the Brazilian contemplative Nuns*, Albano, 3.9.1971. See John Paul II, V., 3; Francis, VDq, 5; 8; 36.

revolutionary spirit. Cultivating the primacy of God, these religious operate a lot for the eternal salvation of souls. But if they accept such as spirit, they will enter into the way of perdition.

> *"The whole work of renewal of the Church, so providentially set forth and initiated by the Second Vatican Council - a renewal that must be both an updating and a consolidation of what is eternal and constitutive of the Church's mission - can be carried out only in the Holy Spirit, that is to say, with the aid of His light and his power."*[32]

Regarding the Constitution VDq and the Instruction *Cor orans*, all the contemplative religious finds themselves in front of a fundamental and epochal decision: remaining faithful to the charisma of their saintly founders, to the Ecumenical Second Vatican Council and to the Holy Ghost, or accepting the new revolutionary spirit that substitutes that of the second Pentecost and leads to the extinction of their religious orders.

> *"Today, we must implore with fervor a great grace from the Holy Ghost. The hour that rings on the clock face of history effectively demands*

---

[32] Saint John Paul II, *Apostolic Letter A Concilio Constantinopolitano I of his Holiness John Paul II to the Bishops of the Catholic Church for the 1600th anniversary of the First Council of Constantinople and the 1550th anniversary of the Council of Ephesus*, 25.3.1981.

from all the sons of the Church a great courage, and in a totally special way the courage of the truth, that the Lord in person recommended to his disciples, when he said: "let your 'yes' mean 'yes' and your 'no' mean 'no' (Mt 5, 37).[33]

This duty of courageously professing the truth is so important that the Lord himself had defined the aim of his coming to this world. In front of Pilate, during the trial that proceeded his condemnation to the Cross, Jesus said these grave words: "I was born for this, I came into the world for this, to bear witness to the truth" (John 18, 37). Jesus is the light of the world (John 8, 12), is the manifestation of the truth: and to complete this mission, from which derives our salvation, Jesus gave his own life, martyr of the truth, that is himself."[34]

In the apocalyptic framework outlined, does the Church not perhaps find itself in mortal danger, similar to Jesus Christ in Gethsemane, while the Apostles slept?[35] The salvific mystery of the Cross of Christ, relived by her in a great and profound manner, will however lead her to a new resurrection with Christ. The Sacred Scriptures predicted an

---

[33] Saint Paul VI, Speech to the College of Cardinals. *The hour of clarity for the faith of the Church*, 18.5.1970.

[34] Saint Paul VI, C. *The courage of truth in the confused present hour*, 20.5.1970. "Any truth, from anyone who said it, comes from the Holy Ghost" (Saint Thomas Aquinas).

[35] See Saint John Paul II, *Homily on Holy Thursday on the missed vigil of the Apostles in Gethsemane and on the actualization of this mysterious event in the Church of today*, 9.4.1992.

extraordinary intervention of the Lord in the Holy Ghost at the end of times:

> *"Lord… make hasten to help me' (Ps 141, 1). It is the cry of someone who feels he is in grave danger but it is also the cry of the Church amid the many threats that surround her, that threaten her holiness (…) which instead must be preserved for the Lord's coming. (…) We await the Lord not in the same way as a beautiful decoration upon a world already saved, but as the only way of liberation from a mortal danger"*.[36]

"The spirit and the bride both say to Jesus, the Lord, 'come!' (see Rev 22, 17)" (LG 4). This is the eschatological breath of the Council, but more than ever of the Church in apocalyptic tribulation: "amen. Come Lord Jesus!" (Rev 22, 20).

By now the return of Christ in glory is near. "The Lord Himself speaks: 'behold I come quickly! And my reward is with me, to render to each one according to his works. I am the Alpha and the Omega, the first and the last, the beginning and the end' (Rev 22, 12-13)" (GD 45, 3).

---

[36] Benedict XVI, *Celebration of First Vespers of the First Sunday of Advent*, 29.11.2008. See Saint Paul VI, C. 13.5. 1970.

TABLE OF CONTENTS

INTRODUCTION 5
LEGEND 12
INSTRUCTION 13
THE FIRST NEED OF THE CHURCH 14
A NEW GRAND ASCENSION 21
THE HOLY GHOST, SOUL OF COMMUNITARIAN LIFE 33
THE RENEWAL IS NOT A REVOLUTION 36
A NEW FORMATION 40
THE GREATEST STRUGGLE OF THE DRAGON 47
AT AN EPOCHAL CROSSROADS 51
TABLE OF CONTENTS 58

www.ingramcontent.com/pod-product-compliance
Lightning Source LLC
LaVergne TN
LVHW011413080426
835511LV00005B/523